KT-546-183

Publishers: Ladybird Books Ltd., Loughborough

'People at Work'

The
ROCK STAR

by J.A. HAZELEY, N.S.F.W.
and J.P. MORRIS, O.M.G.

(Authors of 'Herbie,
 The Very Busy Bassist')

A LADYBIRD BOOK FOR GROWN–UPS

This is a rock star. His name is Bob Dylan.

Bob is rehearsing with his band. It takes a long time.

First the band have to learn all of Bob's famous songs.

Then Bob has to think of worse tunes he can sing over all of them.

Sting is in the Amazon basin looking for ideas for basslines.

Every day, an area of rainforest the size and dampness of Wales is destroyed.

"That forest may have contained a bassline that could save the world," says Sting, wiping away a tear.

Sting is the planet's only hope, thinks Sting.

This hologram of David Bowie has been on tour in the Far East since 2016 as part of the singer's posthumous legacy to his fans.

Next year it will take six months off to work on a new album with a hologram of Brian Eno.

Kate Bush is recording a song she has written, but she is refusing to sing into the microphone.

"I am shy," says Kate Bush. "I do not like singing live."

She has brought some of her old records in. Maybe she could play one of those into the microphone instead. Would that count?

Sir Elton John employs a lot of people who help him get ready to play the piano.

His finger—buffer, his spectacle sommelier, his dandifier, and his dancer—cum—barber.

He also has a lady to point out whoever is talking to him, so Sir Elton will not tire himself out looking around the room.

Will–I–Am is working with an exciting young Somalian yodeller and keytarist he found busking on the Shanghai Metro.

Within a week, the two musicians are working on new material in Will's remote studio.

Or this may all be happening in Will–I–Am's head.

The lady is upset because Peter Gabriel has been hiding in her wall.

"I was recording the sound of wood," says Peter Gabriel.

Aerosmith's contract demands that five copies of the Wall Street Journal are delivered backstage before a show, with every letter 'o' coloured in using a green pen.

The band are not being prima donnas. It is a good way to check the contract has been read, and therefore that the stage is safe.

If the promoter fails, Aerosmith are contractually permitted to hunt him for sport on quad bikes.

Bono is about to do a radio interview in Sydney, but he has left his interview sunglasses on the beach in California.

Now Bono will have to charter a mole machine to tunnel right through the earth's core to get them back.

"I can't be expected to talk about the environment on the radio without my special sunglasses," says Bono.

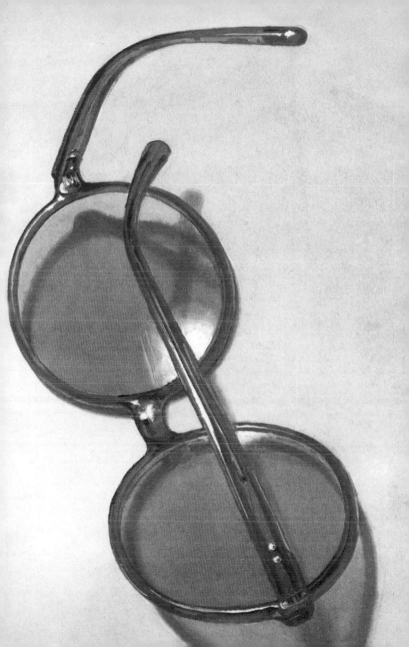

Adele does not like being in an expensive recording studio.

"Studios are well stuck up and posh," says Adele.

She is recording her new album through the switchboard at her local dog food cannery.

"The pies here are brilliant," says Adele.

Even though he is a very busy rock star, Bruce Springsteen does not like to fly in an aeroplane.

When he needs to go to another country, he travels in his private boat.

Today, he has come to London, to buy some Marmite.

Radiohead's friends and families have come to hear them play their new album.

If their friends and families like the record, Radiohead will throw it away and start again.

The Beach Boys have split up.

Mike got the rights to the songs and the name.

And Bruce got the beach.

Dave Grohl of the Foo Fighters is writing out the set–lists for tonight's concert by hand.

He will then tune the guitars, set up the drums, and clean the hotel rooms of all his band and crew, before meeting some fans.

Dave Grohl is the nicest man in rock.

He is definitely up to something.

This special instrument was hand–made for Damon Albarn by a luthier in New Orleans. It cost over $25,000.

Damon refuses to play any other instrument on stage now, or use a microphone.

When someone shouts "Parklife!" Damon kicks his stool over.

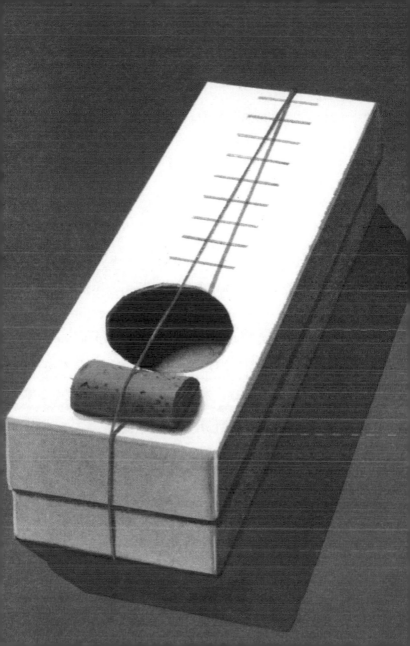

The Icelandic singer Björk is asking her tour manager to stop the bus so she can go and squat in a bush.

Björk's tour bus does have a toilet, but the noise of the flush upsets her backing puffins.

These Pet Shop Boys are working on a record.

To shake up their song–writing habits, they are collaborating with OKTOR, a vintage Hungarian power station computer.

Neil likes OKTOR's suggestion of a skate–metal direction.

Michael Jackson's Neverland ranch had a roller-coaster, a zoo and a genetically engineered giant version of his younger self to make children's dreams come true.

Holger Czukay of the German avant–garde rock band Can is recording his latest album on an exciting new format — steam.

"This song is just right," says Holger.

Now he will seal the box and send it to his record company. They usually work out what to do.

These items recently fetched over $150,000 at auction.

They formed part of the dressing room paraphernalia of the late rock star Prince.

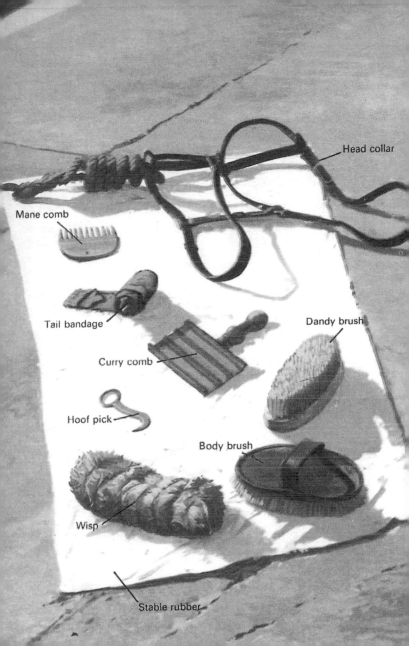

Head collar

Mane comb

Tail bandage

Dandy brush

Curry comb

Hoof pick

Body brush

Wisp

Stable rubber

Kevin Rowland has reformed his band Dexy's Midnight Runners to record his new song about bread.

Kevin is angry that none of the other Midnight Runners want to do the dance he has made up.

This afternoon, Kevin will go solo again.

Some rock stars do not behave like rock stars.

The Scottish group Belle and Sebastian like quiet reading, warm milk and golf.

They were introduced to golf by their friend Alice Cooper.

Paul McCartney is one of the most successful rock stars in the world. But he still travels by train just like anyone else.

This particular train goes from Paul's bathroom to his towel room.

Coldplay's singer Chris Martin has spent weeks working with an important stylist. They have come up with an exciting look for the band's new tour.

"These great clothes make me look really interesting," thinks Chris as he sits down at the piano to practise another slow, sad song that gets slightly louder at the end.

THE AUTHORS would like to record their gratitude and offer their apologies to the many Ladybird artists whose luminous work formed the glorious wallpaper of countless childhoods. Revisiting it for this book as grown-ups has been a privilege.

MICHAEL JOSEPH
UK | USA | Canada | Ireland | Australia
India | New Zealand | South Africa

Michael Joseph is part of the Penguin Random House group of companies whose addresses can be found at global.penguinrandomhouse.com

First published 2017
001

Copyright © Jason Hazeley and Joel Morris, 2017
All images copyright © Ladybird Books Ltd, 2017

The moral right of the authors has been asserted

Printed in Italy by L.E.G.O. S.p.A

A CIP catalogue record for this book is available from the British Library

ISBN: 978-0-718-18865-8

www.greenpenguin.co.uk